ÉVA BENSARD
BENJAMIN CHAUD

THE GREAT BIG BOOK OF MUSEUMS

Translated by
KARIN SNELSON

RED COMET PRESS • BROOKLYN

The Palace Museum
(Beijing, China)

The State Hermitage
(St. Petersburg, Russia)

The Frida Kahlo Museum
(Mexico City, Mexico)

The National Museum of Fine Arts
(Algiers, Algeria)

The American Museum of Natural History
(New York, United States)

The Quai Branly Museum
(Paris, France)

THE VATICAN MUSEUMS IN ROME
Where popes live and collect treasures

It's five in the morning in Rome, Italy . . . already time for Gianni to get ready. Dressed in his navy-blue suit, he gears up to make his rounds. He is the Italian clavigero, the head keeper of the keys, and it's his team who opens the countless doors of the Vatican Museums every single day. His enormous key ring in one hand, a flashlight in the other, Gianni covers miles of Vatican territory. He juggles hundreds of keys, but he never mixes them up. Egyptian sarcophagi, Greek vases, Italian paintings . . . when he flips the light switches, treasure after treasure emerges from the darkness. One of the keys is particularly precious: the one that opens the Sistine Chapel. He can never lose this key; there's only one copy! This chapel, adorned with Italian Renaissance paintings, attracts huge crowds every morning. But Gianni is always the first to lay eyes on it. In this quiet calm he can admire the ceiling painted by Michelangelo. Even after twenty-five-plus years at the Vatican, he's still moved by this wondrous sight. When evening comes, and all the visitors have vanished, he checks every room, making sure nothing has been damaged. Then he locks all the doors again, feeling very lucky to be the Vatican's keeper of the keys.

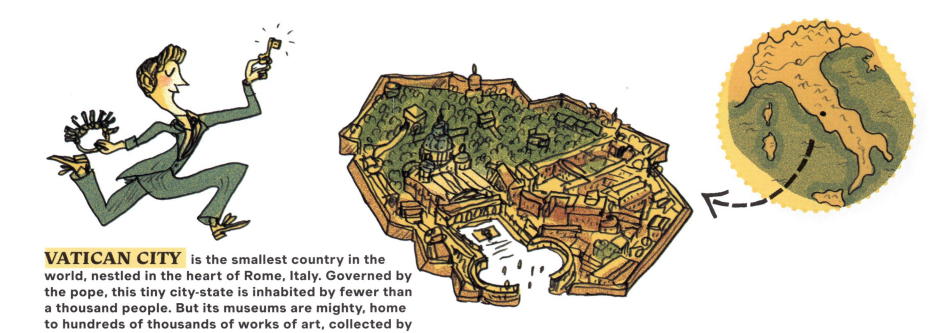

VATICAN CITY is the smallest country in the world, nestled in the heart of Rome, Italy. Governed by the pope, this tiny city-state is inhabited by fewer than a thousand people. But its museums are mighty, home to hundreds of thousands of works of art, collected by the popes over centuries.

Welcome to the Home of the Popes!
During your visit, you may enter the apartments of the popes of the Renaissance and stroll through the same hallways they did. In the sumptuous sixteenth-century Gallery of Maps, the walls are covered with painted maps of the Italian peninsula. This inspiring gallery was commissioned by Pope Gregory XIII, who wanted to travel without ever leaving the walls of the Vatican Palace.

Who was Julius II?
The pope who reigned from 1503 to 1513 was as powerful as an emperor, which earned him the name Julius, after Julius Caesar II. He valued the arts and surrounded himself with Italian geniuses such as Michelangelo and Raphaël.

The Laocoön and His Sons
One lucky day in 1506, in a vineyard near Rome, some winegrowers accidentally unearthed a huge marble sculpture from ancient Greece! The nearly life-sized figures proved to be the Trojan priest Laocoön and his two sons, fighting off monstrous snakes. The pope at that time, Julius II, rushed to buy it, and the Laocoön became the jewel of his collection, proudly displayed in his palace. After him, other popes acquired more and more artwork, eventually transforming the Vatican Palace into a true museum.

★ **Insider Tip**
The dress code inside the Vatican is very strict. Leave your shorts, short skirts, crop tops, and baseball caps in your suitcase!

The Sistine Chapel

This is the highlight of any visit to the Vatican. It is a sacred place where popes are still elected to this day. Once a year, the frescos of its soaring ceiling vaults get dusted, thanks to a "spider lift" with an articulated arm that can reach a height of 66 feet (20 meters). Safe in their baskets, feather dusters in hand, the conservators find themselves nose to nose with 350 figures painted by Michelangelo in the sixteenth century.

Who was Michelangelo?
A Renaissance artist (1475–1564) and master sculptor, born in Florence, Italy. No block of marble could resist him. He could paint, too . . . Just go to the Sistine Chapel and look up.

The powerful gesture in Michelangelo's *The Creation of Adam* has often been appropriated, as in this poster for Steven Spielberg's film *E.T. the Extra-Terrestrial*.

▶ Don't Miss . . .
The Ethnological Museum (*Anima Mundi*) showcases eighty thousand objects from every continent, such as this headdress from Papua New Guinea, almost 9 feet (3 meters) tall. This is Pope Francis's favorite section.

La Scala Momo
Snake your way to the exit! This spiral staircase, or scala, was designed by Italian architect and engineer Giuseppe Momo in 1932. Gaze down upon the sensational, serpentine coil and take a striking photo.

♥ A Souvenir to Bring Home
Stamps issued by the Vatican State are available for purchase in various post offices located inside the museums.

The Vatican Gardens
Popes have been relaxing on sunny lawns and in the shady woods of the Vatican's gardens for seven hundred years, but you will need reservations. The grounds are huge – nearly 57 acres (23 hectares) – taking up half of the Vatican complex. Here, gardeners Massimiliano and Gilberto tend the papal salad greens. It takes more than thirty people to maintain these gardens!

Once upon a time there was a young Canadian boy named Frank Gehry who was so fascinated by fish, mostly carp, that people nicknamed him "Fish." His grandmother bought carp to cook for the Jewish family's traditional Sabbath dinner, and she kept them alive in the bathtub. Frank would watch them twisting and turning in there for hours. Many years later, as an architect living in the US, he translated his childhood obsession with how fish move into one of his most spectacular constructions, the Guggenheim Museum Bilbao, in the Basque Country of north-central Spain. Like a gigantic carp, this building flows along the river, its fins rippling and its silvery skin sparkling. The structure, all curves, surprised everyone. This modern and contemporary art museum was a first of its kind in 1997, attracting one million visitors its very first year. Not bad for a city of around 345,000 residents. Thanks to this continued influx of sightseers, Bilbao is prospering. Shops, hotels, a rapid transit system, and an eco-friendly tram line were built to welcome tourists, and all that has benefited the residents, too: Daily life is more enjoyable, unemployment is down. It's called the Guggenheim Effect. This virtuous circle continues today, to the delight of the residents of Bilbao!

THE GUGGENHEIM MUSEUM BILBAO, designed by Canadian American architect Frank Gehry, rises from the banks of the Nervión River in Bilbao, Spain. To ensure the structural integrity of a design where nearly nothing is straight, he used the same 3-D software employed in the construction of planes and rockets.

Who is Frank Gehry?
Born in Toronto in 1929, Frank moved to Los Angeles, California, in 1947. The Guggenheim Museum Bilbao put him on the world map. He also designed the Museum of Pop Culture in Seattle, Washington.

What's This Museum Made Out Of?

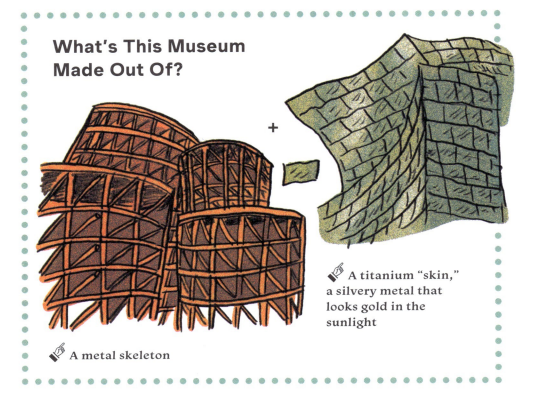

👉 A metal skeleton

👉 A titanium "skin," a silvery metal that looks gold in the sunlight

★ **Insider Tip**
Pintxos (pronounced *pinch-ohss*) are savory toast snacks originating in the Basque region of Spain, served in all the bars of Bilbao and also at the Guggenheim!

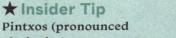

A Rich Family Tradition
For the love of art, Solomon R. Guggenheim (1861–1949) started a trend. This wealthy US industrialist wanted to display his modern art collection, so he commissioned American architect Frank Lloyd Wright to design the flying saucer-like museum that would one day be New York City's Guggenheim. His niece, Peggy Guggenheim (1898–1979), followed in his footsteps, supporting the work of young artists like American painter Jackson Pollock and launching her own art museum in Venice, Italy. Today, the family's foundation continues to help fund museums like the Guggenheim Museum Bilbao.

Men in Black
The guards, with their black suits and earpieces, look like secret agents. They keep the closest watch on one of the museum's most iconic works: a huge 1979 painting of American starlet Marilyn Monroe's face – times 150 – by American pop artist Andy Warhol.

Puppy is the name of a giant sculpture of a little dog, the Guggenheim mascot, almost 40 feet (12 meters) tall, and all abloom with living flowers. This enormous West Highland terrier, created by American artist Jeff Koons, stands guard in front of the museum and greets the visitors eager to snap a photo. A curator is specially appointed to pamper *Puppy*, and gardeners keep a close eye on the flowery "fur." Lucky dog!

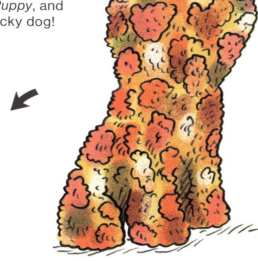

Puppy's colorful coat is made up of thirty-eight thousand living flowers, planted in soil. In the winter, they are mostly blue and purple pansies, and in the summer, pink and red petunias and begonias.

Big Beastie
The museum's other star sculpture is called *Maman*, a giant spider imagined by French American artist Louise Bourgeois as a tribute to her mother, who was also a weaver.

▶ Don't Miss . . .
American sculptor Richard Serra's *The Matter of Time* is a walkable labyrinth. Weighing about 1,300 tons, the tall steel sculpture seems to defy the laws of gravity. Watch out . . . all those curling, tilting metal plates may overwhelm you!

Raising Future Artists
Babies love to mess around with color. The Guggenheim Museum Bilbao offers "Baby Art" workshops, because it's never too early to start painting!

A High-Wire Act
The museum has lighting specialists who use the equipment of a mountain climber . . . essential gear for reaching the dizzying heights of those hard-to-reach lights throughout the building.

🔍 Working Behind the Scenes: Lucia, Exhibition Curator
The Guggenheim Museum Bilbao hosts four exhibitions a year, and Lucia organizes them all. She wears many hats: researching (she loves to champion lesser-known artists), requesting loans of other museums' artwork, getting it safely to Bilbao, and writing catalog copy. She never imagined she'd be able to do all this in her own hometown!

There's no symbol of the United States quite like the Smithsonian Institution . . . and people from around the world visit the capital city of Washington, D.C., to experience the Smithsonian's extraordinary public offerings: fascinating museums, lovely gardens, research centers, libraries — even a zoo and wildlife conservation center — most open seven days a week, fifty-two weeks a year, free of charge!

The Smithsonian Institution is the legacy of James Smithson, a British scientist who, in 1829, bequeathed his fortune to the United States on one condition: that the money be used to spread knowledge far and wide. The complex now includes twenty-one museums and research centers. The first National Museum, founded in 1846, was housed in the Gothic-style Smithsonian Institution Building. Nicknamed "the Castle," it was designed by American architect James Renwick, Jr.

Throughout the twentieth century, the Smithsonian continued to grow, expanding with the National Museum of Natural History, what is now the National Museum of American History, the American Art Museum, the National Portrait Gallery, and more. The National Air and Space Museum and the Hirshhorn Museum and Sculpture Garden were established in the 1970s; the National Museum of the American Indian in the 1990s; and the National Museum of African American History and Culture was inaugurated by President Barack Obama in 2016.

The Smithsonian continues to grow into the twenty-first century with the Museum of the American Latino and the American Women's History Museum.

THE SMITHSONIAN INSTITUTION

is massive! It includes twenty-one museums and research centers that explore American history, art, and culture. Not only that, its scientific research in fields such as human origins, marine biology, species conservation, and space exploration has changed the world.

Many of the Smithsonian's museums are located on the National Mall in Washington, D.C., a 2-mile-long (3 kilometer) green space sometimes called "America's Front Yard." It stretches from the Lincoln Memorial on the banks of the Potomac River to the U.S. Capitol.

But that's not all! The Smithsonian's reach extends past the National Mall to two museums in New York and the Udvar-Hazy Center in Virginia, as well as to research facilities and collaborative partnerships in Boston, Panama, Chile, Hawaii, Arizona, Africa, and beyond.

The Wright brothers designed this extra-light biplane that made the first-ever powered flight in 1903.

Who was James Smithson? Smithson was an English chemist born in 1765. He loved minerals, too: Smithsonite was named for him. Inspired by the values of freedom and equality represented by the French and American revolutions, he bequeathed his fortune to the United States in 1829 to benefit all people with the gift of knowledge. His wish was respected, and the Smithsonian Institution he founded is now world renowned.

Get Ready for Take-Off!
The National Air and Space Museum is a superstar of the Smithsonian, one of the most visited museums in the world. You'll find fun, interactive exhibits and halls full of planes, rockets, spaceships, and all manner of flying objects . . . each shedding light on the history and science of aviation. Some of the tour guides are actual pilots!

The capsule of the American *Apollo 11* spacecraft, which carried the first men to the moon in 1969.

Save the Ferrets
Did you know that the Smithsonian's National Zoo & Conservation Biology Institute help save wildlife species from extinction? Scientists study and breed more than twenty species at their headquarters, including the black-footed ferret and scimitar-horned oryx. They collaborate with colleagues in twenty-five countries around the world and train budding conservationists, too.

🔍 Working Behind the Scenes: Lisa, Spacesuit Specialist
Lisa is an objects conservator at the National Air and Space Museum. Her work is not much different from that of archaeologists who conserve mummies. Lisa's biggest challenge: to conserve the suit of Neil Armstrong, the first man to walk on the moon. Manufactured by NASA, the suit was made of twenty-one layers of state-of-the-art synthetic materials and there is still lunar dust inside the outer fibers!

Tracing the Black American Story

The National Museum of African American History and Culture, which opened in 2016, tells the often neglected, misunderstood, or forgotten stories of Black Americans and their contributions to history. The museum's unusual architecture leads visitors up from the dark days of the Mid-Atlantic slave trade, the American Civil War, and Jim Crow, through the triumphs (and terrors) of the Civil Rights Movement, then on to the explosive effect of Black artists and athletes on popular music, culture, and sports, and into the present day with dynamic exhibitions and objects. Be sure and check out singer and guitarist Chuck Berry's candy-apple red Cadillac.

This architectural marvel on the National Mall was designed by Ghanaian British David Adjaye and American architect Philip Freelon.

The National Museum of African American History and Culture's three-tiered, inverted pyramid shape is reminiscent of a Yoruba crown from West Africa.

After escaping from a Maryland plantation in 1849, Harriet Tubman organized the escape of dozens of slaves, risking her life. See her hymnal and a lace shawl that was gifted to her by England's Queen Victoria.

History Isn't Over

What do President Lincoln's top hat, a life jacket from the *Titanic*, Dorothy's ruby slippers from *The Wizard of Oz*, and the droids from *Star Wars* have in common? They are all on display in the Smithsonian National Museum of American History! Each of the hundreds of thousands of objects in the collection has a story to tell about American history and popular culture.

★ Insider Tip

The National Museum of Natural History is an endless treasure trove of wonders, including the (allegedly) cursed Hope Diamond and the O. Orkin Insect Zoo. If you are not afraid of big hairy spiders (and even if you are, a little), you can witness a tarantula's lunch.

▶ Don't Miss . . .

Discover the famous *Number 3, 1949: Tiger* by acclaimed American painter (and paint flinger) Jackson Pollock and the work of other contemporary artists at the Hirshhorn Museum on the National Mall.

The Faces of History

Located just off the National Mall, the National Portrait Gallery paints a picture of American history with the individuals who have shaped its culture, from George Washington to Josephine Baker. The museum hosts the nation's only complete collection of presidential portraits outside the White House, along with portraits of poets, artists, visionaries, actors, and activists.

Sporting a big, floppy straw hat, Charlotte could easily be mistaken for a sun-sensitive tourist on vacation. But that wouldn't explain the unusual pouch on her belt. "That's for my pruning shears," she explains. "An essential tool when you're in charge of the Mucem garden!" The Mucem? A museum dedicated to Mediterranean cultures in sunny Marseille, a culturally diverse port city in southern France, right on the Mediterranean Sea. Since the Mucem's opening in 2013, newcomers and regulars have mingled on its footbridges, on its rooftop terrace, and in its galleries, where the exhibits explore major changes and trends in society. For example, the memorable *We Are Soccer* exhibit was a tribute to the round ball with the power to bring a neighborhood together or even unite an entire city . . . from Paris to Marseille, Algiers to Athens! The Mucem is also home to a golden-hued garden, a touch of beautifully planned wildness atop the historic Fort Saint-Jean. "It's crazy how the trees have grown! We even organized an olive harvest with the help of the locals," Charlotte raves. Some Marseille residents visit the Mediterranean garden daily, picnicking in the shade of the olive trees or enjoying the panoramic views of the blue water, all the while lulled by cicada songs. In the middle of this shrubby little oasis, the big city feels far away . . .

THE MUCEM is short for the Museum of European and Mediterranean Civilizations. Its two distinct buildings sit on the French coast of the Mediterranean Sea: Fort Saint-Jean, a twelfth-century Louis XIV-era fortress, and the J4, an ultra-modern cube designed by French architects Rudy Ricciotti and Roland Carta.

Who is Rudy Ricciotti? Born in Algeria in 1952, this French architect and engineer was introduced to construction by his father, a mason. Influenced by Mediterranean culture and driven by a zeal for technical challenges, Rudy earned international acclaim for his stylish Mucem design.

Suspended above the sea like a flying carpet—no cables!—this narrow 377-foot-long (115 meter) footbridge links the two Mucem buildings.

Night Show, Light Show
When night falls, the Mucem glows with turquoise lights, a tribute to the powerful blue sea by contemporary French artist Yann Kersalé.

Concrete Lace
What is the coral-like pattern covering the modern J4 building? Made of ultra-resistant concrete, these lacy walls are both elegant and useful: They filter the sun, much like the wooden latticework in Arabic mashrabiyas.

Surprising Stuff
In this "museum of society," you'll find it all: Snow globes sit next to old farming tools, kitchen utensils, and marionettes . . . and there's a ball from the Olympique de Marseille soccer club! The Mucem reveals how our belongings can be a window into our lifestyles, our hobbies, and even our beliefs.

Street Art
The Mucem celebrates contemporary urban culture in all its expressions, including graffiti-covered objects and painted skateboards.

All Aboard!

It's not always easy to get to the museum, even for those living in Marseille. Luckily, a free Sunday bus program called "Destination Mucem" services the outlying districts. Once on board, a friendly guide welcomes families and offers them museum tickets, too.

★ **Insider Tip**
The Mucem is among the top fifty most visited museums in the world. It's been a game-changer for Marseille, introducing new tourists to the beauty of the city. Above all, the Mucem is a source of pride for the locals, who account for nearly a third of its visitors.

▶ **Don't Miss . . .**
La Belle de Mai is an old Marseille neighborhood, now home to the Mucem Center for Conservation and Resources (CCR), where the public can see thousands of curiosities on metal shelving, from bread shaped like a mermaid to a fortune-telling machine.

Top Chef

The Mucem's vegetable garden tells a tale of Mediterranean vegetables: tomatoes, zucchini, peppers, eggplant . . . all the makings of ratatouille. Every morning, the gardeners harvest a basket of fresh produce for the acclaimed French chef Gérald Passedat, who opened a restaurant and cooking school at the Mucem.

🔍 **Working Behind the Scenes: Marianne, Collections Photographer**
Marianne patiently documents the Mucem's collections in her photo studio, from carousel horses to small Nativity figurines from Provence. She loves learning about the history of each special item. Her challenge? To bring these inanimate artifacts to life by playing around with the lighting. "A trick of the light can bring magic to the most ordinary object!" she says.

THE RIJKSMUSEUM IN AMSTERDAM
A magnificent time machine

A museum with a bicycle path running right through it? Only in the Netherlands, a land even more famous for its bicycles than for its round cheeses, do the bikes outnumber the people — twenty-three million per seventeen million residents! In Amsterdam, cyclists are buzzing around everywhere, but it's still surprising to see them making a beeline toward the elegant, red-bricked Rijksmuseum, then calmly heading straight into the building. As they slow down, they can even see all the visitors through the windows. Thousands of them wander the floors of this historic "royal museum" every day.

The tourists flock to see Dutch master Vermeer's *The Milkmaid*, an industrious young woman unfazed by her many admirers. This oil painting, along with many other works, transports them to the heart of the Golden Age, the seventeenth century, a time when the Netherlands was a great trading power. Its fast ships traded with the whole world, and Amsterdam was a dazzlingly prosperous port city. A ticket to the Rijksmuseum (pronounced *Rikes*, rhymes with *bikes*) is like a personal invitation to the opulent Dutch homes of this era, filled with paintings, Oriental rugs, and musical instruments. Veilige reis! Have a nice trip!

THE "RIJKS" opened its doors in 1885. At that time, it was the largest building in the Netherlands, impressive inside and out. Its Dutch architect, Pierre Cuypers, specialized in churches, and that passion clearly spilled out into the Rijksmuseum's stained-glass windows, mosaics, and vaulted cathedral ceilings.

★ **Insider Tip**
Women painters, including Dutch artist Judith Leyster, added their own shine to the Golden Age . . . and to the Rijks's Gallery of Honor. Here is Leyster's *Jolly Toper* (1629).

"Made in the Netherlands"

The Rijksmuseum galleries — with eight thousand works — retrace eight hundred years of Dutch history and unfold chronologically. The second floor is devoted to the seventeenth century. Here are a few must-haves of the Golden Age:

✑ Commission a painting! *Portrait of a Married Couple* by Dutch Master Frans Hals

✑ Just add tulips! A pyramid vase from Delft, a Dutch town known for its blue-and-white porcelain

✑ A lavish doll house: *the* toy for fancy ladies

Who was Vermeer?
Dutch master Vermeer (1632–1675) painted only thirty or so paintings in his lifetime, but that was enough to make him a star. Not much is known about him, but thanks to his work, we have a window into the seventeenth-century lives and homes of the Dutch people . . . seeing them up close, perhaps imagining their secret thoughts.

Operation Night Watch

Like moths to a flame, visitors are drawn to Dutch master Rembrandt's painting *The Night Watch* (1642). This group portrait—nearly 15 feet (4.5 meters) wide—represents a band of civic guardsmen armed with spears and guns, ready to protect and defend Amsterdam. Almost four hundred years old, this painting was showing its age. But instead of sending it to the lab, the conservators came to the painting: These experts work their magic in the public eye, inside a state-of-the-art glass chamber.

Who was Rembrandt? Dutch master Rembrandt (1606–1669), painter and printmaker, spent most of his career in Amsterdam. Here, he became famous for his talent for portraits and his exquisite use of light and shadow.

▶ **Don't Miss . . .**
The Model Ship Gallery on the ground floor is a favorite of Dutch schoolchildren, and features eighteen hundred ship models of all sorts, as well as figureheads large and small, all beautiful.

♥ **A Souvenir to Take Home**
A free sketchbook awaits you at the reception rotunda! Is there a painting you like? Break out your pencil—also free—and sketch away. Our suggestion to get started: Dutch painter Hendrick Avercamp's *Winter Landscape with Ice Skaters* (1608).

Tulip Mania

If the Netherlands were a flower, it would be a tulip! Most of the world's tulips are grown here, a tradition dating back to the 1600s. At that time, this flower was rare and a sign of wealth: You'll spot tulip motifs all over the Rijksmuseum's art collection. To see a huge variety of tulips in real life, visit the museum's gardens in April when they're blooming by the hundreds.

Find the Van Gogh . . .
Dutch master Vincent van Gogh (1853–1890) has his very own museum in Amsterdam. But if you keep your eyes peeled, you can find one of his self-portraits at the Rijks, amidst a fine collection of modern paintings.

🔍 **Working in Plain Sight: Annika, Museum Guide**
Annika knows the Rijksmuseum inside and out and helps visitors discover the museum's masterpieces. Her favorite painter? Vermeer! She adores the atmosphere of his paintings, where time seems to stop. She's a true art lover, speaks several languages, and always happy to share what she knows.

THE LOUVRE IN PARIS
An epic journey through art history

As she does every morning, Dorine fetches her art supplies from a hidden cabinet in the Louvre. She retrieves her canvas, a large wooden easel, and a stool, and sets up in front of "her" painting, a ravishing Italian Madonna. She pulls the colorful paint tubes out of her bag, along with some brushes and a rag. She's ready to get to work! "You have to apply the oil paint in very thin layers, like the masters of the past," the student explains, delighted to perfect her brushstrokes in such a prestigious venue. One day, she'd like to restore paintings professionally.

A few rooms away, Tianshu is at work in front of *The Bolt*, a famous painting by French artist Jean-Honoré Fragonard.

The Louvre is the "best school in the world," says this young Chinese woman who came to Paris to study Western painting techniques. Like Dorine, she is one of the lucky few allowed set up her easel on the Louvre floor for a few months and copy a painting. Of course, the visiting painters must remain faithful to the original artists' techniques and not forge their signatures! Curious museumgoers have started to gather around the two students. Some will return in a few weeks to admire their progress. In the meantime, many surprises await these visitors to the awe-inspiring Louvre — the largest museum in the world — where age-old paintings hang alongside the French crown jewels, and the Winged Victory of Samothrace is a neighbor of the *Mona Lisa*.

THE LOUVRE was originally a fortified castle for French kings, built in Paris around 1200. That fortress was destroyed, and only part of the old moat endures. You can cross it today—and stay dry!—on your way to the Egyptian rooms.

Who was I. M. Pei?
Chinese American architect Ieoh Ming Pei (1917–2019) was born in China, and has designed sleek, often geometric buildings in the US and around the world. His metal-and-glass pyramid at the Louvre—the museum's dramatic entrance as of 1989—was constructed using 675 glass panels.

A Tradition of Change
The Louvre has evolved enormously in eight hundred years. Post-fortress, it was a royal palace, then became a public museum in 1793, after the French Revolution. Architects have expanded and embellished it over time, and not without scandal. I. M. Pei's modern pyramid has been criticized by many, but now it's iconic. Today, the Louvre attracts around nine million visitors a year.

Three Superstars

Mona Lisa (or *La Joconde*)
Italian beauty painted by Leonardo da Vinci (Italy, circa 1503)

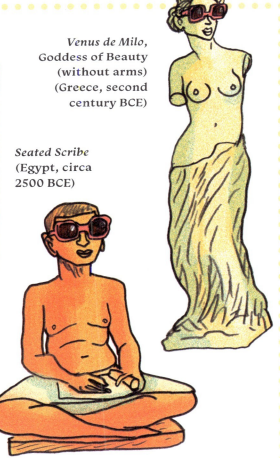

Venus de Milo, Goddess of Beauty (without arms) (Greece, second century BCE)

Seated Scribe (Egypt, circa 2500 BCE)

★ Insider Tip
Visit the Apollo Gallery, commissioned by the young Louis XIV, the Sun King. Its grand, gilded decor was a model for the Hall of Mirrors in the royal palace of Versailles, outside of Paris.

Thousands of Paintings . . .
Italy, the Netherlands, Spain—the Louvre's paintings come from all over Europe. France, too, of course! In room after room, the history of French painting unfolds, from the Middle Ages to the nineteenth century. A must-see: Eugène Delacroix's *Liberty Leading the People* (1830), a huge painting that embodies the French revolutionary spirit.

A Louvre Groove
Beyoncé and Jay-Z made a music video singing and dancing among the Louvre's most famous works from the *Mona Lisa* to the Winged Victory of Samothrace. The museum even customized a seventeen-stop tour!

Their video also spotlights a portrait of a Black woman, rare in Western art history, painted in 1800 by French artist Marie-Guillemine Benoist (1768–1826).

An Egyptian Journey
Spanning five thousand years of history, the Louvre's massive display of more than six thousand Egyptian works inspires Egyptologists worldwide. The highlight: the collection of sarcophagi. In these comfortable "sleeping cases," the deceased could complete their voyages to the great beyond . . . after mummification, that is.

▶ Don't Miss . . .
In Near Eastern Antiquities: remnants from the Palace of Darius I at Susa (now Iran). The brick walls teem with soldiers. Weapons at the ready, archers—from 510 BCE—symbolically guarded the Persian king's palace.

The Louvre School
Art enthusiasts have been studying on the grounds of the Louvre since its school was founded in 1882. The higher education curriculum—now including art history, anthropology, and archaeology—attracts students from all backgrounds and countries. Imagine a world-class museum as your classroom, along with many other Parisian museums!

♥ A Souvenir to Take Home
Children can embark on a museum scavenger hunt with the fun "Louvre passport." Ask for one at the information desk under the pyramid.

THE OCEANOGRAPHIC MUSEUM IN MONACO

Diving 20,000 leagues under the sea

It's stuck like a barnacle to the side of the Rock of Monaco: a sheer cliff that drops straight into the Mediterranean Sea. It took eleven years to build this monumental stone palace, designed by French architect Paul Delefortrie. The ambitious project—the Oceanographic Museum—was the brainchild of seafaring scientist Prince Albert I of Monaco, more than 110 years ago. (Monaco, by the way, is an independent country surrounded by France.)

Today, the Oceanographic Museum is famous for its aquariums, among the oldest in the world. It harbors some hidden-away places, too, such as the marine species care center, created in 2019! Here, teams of expert caretakers work to heal injured turtles found off the coast of Monaco. Some are accidentally trapped in fishing nets, others damaged by boats . . . but all are placed under the close surveillance of careful handlers. When the turtles have regained enough strength, the agile swimmers are transported into a viewable open-air pool where they can recover, delighting museum visitors. Once fully rehabilitated, the turtles are released into the open sea.

Olivier, head sea life caretaker, will always remember the day he said goodbye to Rana. This baby loggerhead turtle was found in the port of Monaco, floating and weak, so small she could fit into the palm of your hand. Four years later and nearly 50 pounds (23 kilos) heavier, Rana was able to rediscover her life in the wild and the path to freedom.

THE OCEANOGRAPHIC MUSEUM

in Monaco was founded in 1910 by Prince Albert I, who wanted to share his discoveries about the miraculous ocean depths, then little known to the public. Building this cliffside palace was a titanic challenge! Rising from the Mediterranean Sea to its rooftop height of 278 feet (85 meters), the museum is an architectural marvel.

Who was Prince Albert I of Monaco? A prince with sea legs, Albert I (1848–1922) devoted his life to studying the oceans. He led twenty-eight exploration missions on his lab-equipped yachts, all helping pioneer a whole new science: oceanography. His great-great-grandson, Albert II, is driven by the same passion, and continues his fight to protect the oceans.

Jellyfish Chandeliers

From the entrance gates to the mosaic-tile floors to the light fixtures above, the museum's decor teems with tentacles. Drawings by German biologist Ernst Haeckel (1834–1919) served as the model for the incredible jellyfish chandeliers worthy of a Jules Verne novel!

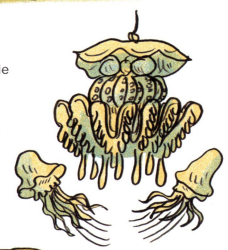

The Aquariums

In the museum's basement, the sea creatures come to life: The octopuses unfurl their tentacles, and the jellyfish show off their tutus! In ninety glorious tanks, visitors will discover the enormous Shark Lagoon, hundreds of Mediterranean species, and tropical corals.

🖎 The oldest aquarium resident is a moray eel, found off the coast of Antibes (on the French Riviera) in 1968. She has earned the right to a tank all to herself, only natural for Madame Moray.

★ Insider Tip

To support the museum and help save the oceans, you can sponsor—for one year—a small dogfish shark, a jellyfish, a Banggai cardinalfish, a golden seahorse, or a clown fish.

A Giant Whale Skeleton

You'll feel like you're inhaling briny sea air with all the nautical paintings, tropical seashells, oceanographic instruments, and thousands of other marine objects around you. At the museum, you're on a voyage where art meets science. One of its top attractions is a giant fin whale skeleton, whose three tons of bones float above your head in the Whale Room.

▶ Don't Miss . . .

Head upstairs to "Oceanomania" to find a floor-to-ceiling display of rare and unusual objects, hand-selected from the museum's historic collection by contemporary New York artist Mark Dion: a stuffed polar bear (caught by Albert I), fossil fish, ship models, and strange diving suits. The result: a giant, uniquely significant cabinet of curiosities dedicated to the sea.

Welcome to the Nursery

Tucked away with the basement aquariums is a nursery of a hundred special tanks where wee sea creatures are born every year: seahorses as tiny as the head of a pin, immature clown fish, cuttlefish, and more, all under the close supervision of specialized technicians called aquariologists, or aquarists.

Klingert's Diving Machine

The first diving suits were highly experimental! This one from 1797, designed by German inventor Karl Heinrich Klingert, allowed a river diver to breath underwater for several minutes at a depth of about 21 feet (6 meters).

The Beloved Jacques Cousteau

Just look for the red cap! Inventor of the Aqua-Lung and the "diving saucer," French underwater explorer Jacques-Yves Cousteau (1910–1997) directed Monaco's Oceanographic Museum for thirty-one years, from 1957 to 1988. Thanks to his documentaries and TV shows, millions of children continue to discover the wonders of the undersea world.

"**W**atch Out for Cats!" You might be surprised to see this sign posted outside Russia's largest museum . . . but St. Petersburg residents say they don't pay much attention to it anymore. They already know the Hermitage basement is crawling with them! Louchka, Mavrik, and, of course, Charlotka are only three of the sixtyish cats that frolic freely in the museum's underground passages. Here, their every desire is met: cozy baskets, bowls of dry food, and even a clinic.

This feline presence is nothing new. The first cats were introduced in the eighteenth century when the Hermitage was the residence of the tsars, the powerful Russian emperors. These kitty-cats of yore were charged with hunting the pesky mice that might nibble on supplies or infest the palace's works of art: masterpieces, precious stones, antique coins. Today, the resident cats are no longer allowed in the imperial halls reserved for two-legged tourists, but they are still quite pampered. In fact, these friendly furballs are getting so popular, they almost steal the show from the other Hermitage stars, namely Leonardo da Vinci, Matisse, and Picasso. You can buy cat-themed souvenirs in the city's shops, and every spring, the museum dedicates a two-day festival to them! Purrs all around . . .

THE HERMITAGE in December, with its snow-dusted facades, looks like something straight out of a Christmas story. Of the Hermitage's five public museum buildings, the eighteenth-century Winter Palace is the most important. Designed by Italian architect Francesco Bartolomeo Rastrelli, it was the former residence of the tsars, rising majestically from the banks of the Neva River that flows through St. Petersburg, Russia.

Bundle up, friends! Russian winters are brutally cold (sometimes even -32° F/-35° C). Workers regularly need to clear the snow-covered roof of the Winter Palace, teetering like tightrope walkers past the 176 statues lining its edge.

Make a Grand Entrance
The Winter Palace still radiates imperial splendor, and the showy Jordan Staircase (1762) is a stellar example. In the eighteenth century, this inviting entryway dazzled ambassadors from all over Europe. Today, it's the tourists who are stunned by its gilded glamor and glittering chandeliers!

The Hermitage Darlings
Dürer, Caravaggio, Gauguin, Monet, Cézanne . . . The Hermitage is home to sixteen thousand paintings, the largest collection in the world. With a few obvious favorites:

1. Matisse *(36 paintings)*
2. Picasso *(31 paintings)*
3. Rembrandt *(23 paintings)*

★ Insider Tip
The Hermitage is the second largest museum in the world. It's so big, it sometimes takes employees twenty minutes to walk to their offices. The staff says there are two types of people: those who work at the museum and those who can't find the exit!

A Very Precious Egg
The tsars went wild for these Fabergé eggs, amazingly ornate Easter eggs encrusted with diamonds and pearls, crafted by a Russian jeweler named . . . Fabergé.

Catherine II, Compulsive Shopper

At the end of the eighteenth century, the Hermitage was overflowing with treasures. The tsarina wanted to outdo the kings of Europe, so she went on a spending spree, admitting: "It's not about the art, it's greed. I am a glutton." Today, the "Russian Louvre" houses three million items, from ancient statues to modern paintings. As you stroll past the endless halls of armor, jewelry, and coins, you'll hardly know where to look!

Voltaire in a Chair

In 1781, Catherine II hired French sculptor Jean-Antoine Houdon to carve this grand marble statue of her friend, French philosopher Voltaire. Even in stone, the artist captures the mischievous gleam in the eye of this Enlightenment-era thinker.

Who was Catherine II? Born a Prussian princess, she dethroned her husband Peter III and—as Catherine the Great—ruled the Russian Empire for thirty-four years (1762–1796). Passionate about studying other cultures and open to new ideas, she created schools throughout the land to combat illiteracy.

Topless *Mona Lisa*

The Hermitage proudly owns two Madonna paintings by Italian artist Leonardo da Vinci, of *Mona Lisa* fame. This less clothed *Mona Lisa* is said to be his student's work.

▶ Don't Miss . . .

It may be 250 years old, but the *Peacock Clock*, crafted by British inventor James Cox, still works. When a curator winds it up, the owl twirls, the peacock fans its tail, and the rooster crows its most joyful cock-a-doodle-do.

🔍 Working Behind the Scenes: Mikhail, Head of Volunteer Services

Volunteers come from all over the world to do internships at the Hermitage: They help greet visitors and set up exhibitions. Mikhail created this program twenty years ago so that younger generations could learn about how the museum functions . . . and so they could infuse their energy and ideas into the Hermitage. His big idea is working!

Dawn breaks over Jingshan Park, in the heart of Beijing. It's early, but the first tourists are already rushing to climb this lush green hill. They've come for the breathtaking views of the Forbidden City, the vast, fifteenth-century palace compound where China's emperors lived for five hundred years. Like a mirage, the ancient wooden buildings with yellow-tiled pagoda roofs stretch as far as the eye can see. Today, the last emperor is long gone, and the "Old Palace" is now the Palace Museum, bursting with wondrous artifacts.

It's hard to imagine that only one hundred years ago the Forbidden City was an impenetrable fortress where the Emperor of China, his ministers, concubines, and countless servants lived. The moats did their job, and access was denied to anyone outside the court, under penalty of death! Times have definitely changed: Now you'll see eager visitors, not guards, and museum conservators, not imperial officials. The Palace Museum's monumental architecture and priceless collections — including hundreds of thousands of ceramics, precious fabrics, paintings, and furniture — allow millions each year to experience the once secretive imperial court.

THE PALACE MUSEUM IN BEIJING
The Forbidden City of China's emperors

THE PALACE MUSEUM—

built between 1406 and 1420—was once Beijing's Forbidden City of neighborhoods, streets, and courtyards . . . sprawling behind a fortified wall nearly 2 miles (around 3 kilometers) long. Over five centuries, twenty-four emperors lived here, including the brilliant Kangxi. Since 1925, the city has become an esteemed museum of Chinese art and artifacts.

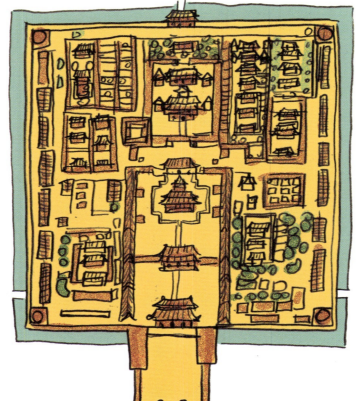

Who was Kangxi?
Fourth emperor of the Qing Dynasty, Kangxi governed for sixty-one years, from 1661 to 1722. A scholarly ruler, he loved art, literature, and the sciences. His reign is sometimes compared to that of King Louis XIV, his contemporary in France.

Marching Orders!
To fully explore this immense city, comfortable walking shoes are essential. You'll see the staff riding around on bicycles. It's faster and less exhausting!

★ Insider Tip
About fifteen hundred people work at the Palace Museum. Conservators closely monitor the condition of their precious collections, as well as the buildings, always in need of renovation. In 2018, an ultra-modern, high-tech "relic hospital" was built to repair damaged artifacts.

The National Treasure
People will line up for hours to see *Along the River During the Qingming Festival*, the much-revered, one-thousand-year-old painted silk scroll measuring a staggering 17.3 feet (5.28 meters) long. Here, Song Dynasty landscape painter Zhang Zeduan elegantly chronicles a river scene from medieval China, its shores bustling with villagers from all walks of life. This painting is so fragile, it's rarely exhibited.

The Hall of Supreme Harmony

Unmatched in the city in both splendor and size, this superb hall is 115 feet (35 meters) tall. Here, enthroned emperors watched grand ceremonies, coronations, and weddings. What a glorious, movie-ready setting! Italian director Bernardo Bertolucci was the first to film inside the palace walls, and *The Last Emperor* (1987) tells the incredible story of the young ruler Puyi (1906–1967).

Who was Puyi?
Born in 1906, he was a child emperor by age three and soon caught up in a whirlwind of history. In 1911, the people revolted and proclaimed a Republic—no more emperors! Puyi was the last emperor of China. He fought but failed to restore the imperial regime.

▶ **Don't Miss . . .**
Explore beyond the overcrowded "central axis" of the palace grounds. Once you're off the beaten path, you'll experience an entirely different city, surprisingly quiet and deserted. The fabulous Nine-Dragon Wall—with nine different carved dragons on a sea of blue tiles—is worth a visit to the northwest sector.

Chinese emperors were considered "Sons of Heaven," and their symbol was the dragon. Painted, engraved, or sculpted, this celestial beast appears in every nook and cranny of the city: on the walls, doors, beams, and tiles. Its sinewy, scaly body slithers upon countless museum objects as well, from porcelain vases to embroidered imperial robes.

Fire Drill
Fire is the number one enemy of this city built almost entirely of wood. The museum is prepared: They have five thousand fire extinguishers and an onsite fire brigade, on call twenty-four hours a day.

Long Live the Happy Couple!
Lovebirds flock to the museum for wedding photographs, especially the fortified outer walls and the moat. In China, traditional wedding dresses are not white but red, the Chinese color of luck and happiness.

THE NATIONAL MUSEUM OF FINE ARTS IN ALGIERS
Bridging two Mediterranean shores

Nineteenth-century European painters were fascinated by the Arab Maghreb lands of northern Africa — some of them French colonies at that time. Without modern-day airplane travel, however, it took artists weeks or even months to reach the Maghreb, by boat across the Mediterranean Sea, then on horses, and on the backs of camels. Parisian artist Eugène Delacroix was one of the first to tackle this adventure. The hundreds of drawings he brought back with him to France continued to inspire him his whole life. After him, other Western painters attempted the journey and were just as thrilled by the sandy landscapes, white-walled cities, and fine Islamic craftsmanship.

Today, you'll find some of these European travelers' paintings on display at the National Museum of Fine Arts in Algiers (Algeria's capital), home to one of the largest art collections in Africa. The museum also celebrates Arab artists, such as Algerian painter Mohammed Racim (1896–1975). He is known for his talent as a miniaturist, his ability to transform a simple piece of paper into a storybook world as enchanting as *The Book of 1001 Nights*. Through his colorful, exquisitely detailed paintings, you can imagine slipping through the busy narrow streets of Algiers or climbing onto the roof terraces of the Casbah, where women chat and brew mint tea in the light of the setting sun.

THE NATIONAL MUSEUM OF FINE ARTS

in Algiers (Algeria), with its geometric shapes and simple white facades, was on the cutting edge of modernity when it opened in 1931. French architect Paul Guion was inspired by the Art Deco style, then all the rage in Europe. The best part: a panoramic terrace, overlooking the resplendent Bay of Algiers.

Impressive Impressionists

Built by French colonists, the museum initially focused on buying lots of European paintings. Its first director wanted to show the evolution of Western art since the Renaissance, and the nineteenth century was not forgotten: Impressionist-era paintings by Monet, Pissarro, and Gauguin made the trip to Algiers, too.

An Independent Algeria

After eight years of war with France, Algeria gained independence in 1962 and asserted its cultural identity. Arab art abounds at the museum, including an entire floor dedicated to twentieth-century Algerian artists such as Baya, known for her joyful, colorful paintings.

Who was Baya?
Algerian artist Baya Mahieddine (1931–1998) creates a playful, dreamlike universe of women, flora, fauna, fairy tales, and folk art. Orphaned young in Algiers, she eventually found a home with a wealthy French art collector who recognized her talent, had excellent Parisian connections, and encouraged her to paint. At sixteen years old, she was already a star, championed by the likes of Matisse and Picasso.

Traveling Painters

The Heart of the Desert
In 1883, Parisian artist Étienne Dinet ventured farther south to the Sahara Desert . . . and was utterly spellbound. He grew deeply attached to Algeria, learned Arabic, moved to Bou Saada, converted to Islam, and changed his name to Nasreddine Dinet. His warm paintings vividly capture the daily lives of the villagers and the nomadic Bedouin tribes.

A Pioneer
When French painter Eugène Delacroix arrived in northern Africa in 1832, everything amazed him: Arabian horses and their proud riders, brilliantly colorful fabrics, traditional holidays. He couldn't sketch it all fast enough. In Western art, this fantastical (sometimes stereotypical) view of the people and lands of the Eastern "Orient" soon gained a name . . . Orientalism.

Love at First Sight
In the twentieth century, another French artist became "Algerian at heart": landscape painter Albert Marquet (1875–1947). He fell in love with the white walls of Algiers, its port, and also one of its residents, Marcelle! They married in 1923, and Algeria became his second homeland. The country's natural beauty inspired his wonderful paintings of the sea and beyond.

★ Insider Tip
At the foot of the museum, a huge green carpet rolls out to the sea: plantain trees, palms, and giant bamboos. This is the Test Garden of Hamma, one of the most beautiful in Africa. You can still see the old tree with ropelike roots used for swinging (while yelling) in the original 1932 film *Tarzan the Ape Man*.

▶ Don't Miss . . .
Hercules the Archer was first created in 1909 by French sculptor Antoine Bourdelle. Who needs unnecessary details like arrows or a quiver? This artist concentrated instead on the dynamic stance of the mythological Greek hero, who is pushing against a rock to bend his bow.

Miniatures for Mini-Artists
Among many child-friendly activities at the museum, budding artists can try their hand at miniature painting using extra-fine brushes, a technique very popular in Arab-Muslim art.

THE FRIDA KAHLO MUSEUM IN MEXICO CITY
La Casa Azul—a colorful blue sanctuary

Her gaze was frank and intense, her dramatic eyebrows, unforgettable. Add a flower crown — dark braids piled atop her head and intertwined with fresh blossoms — and the portrait is complete. Twentieth-century Mexican artist Frida Kahlo's face is everywhere: on purses, calendars, painted on fingernails. There's even a Frida Barbie. And movie! Would this revolutionary and feminist artist have appreciated all the fuss? We'll never know. One thing is certain: Frida Kahlo is as famous as any pop star. But who was she really? To find out, there's a special place well known to Mexico City locals . . . the blue house . . . La Casa Azul in Spanish.

Frida spent much of her childhood within these warm, comforting walls. Here, she deepened her artistic talents and set up her own studio. She surrounded herself with objects from her homeland that crept into her bold, deeply personal paintings: pottery, embroidered fabrics, statuettes, kitchen utensils. She transformed her garden into a Mexican jungle, bursting with tropical plants, burbling fountains, and curious animals. Today, her little spider monkey, parrots, and hairless dogs (an old Aztec breed) no longer frolic among the courtyard's cacti and colorful flowers, but nothing else has really changed. So, let's push open the door and enter the vivacious realm of Queen Frida!

LA CASA AZUL was built in the historic Coyoacán neighborhood of Mexico City by Frida Kahlo's father, who was a photographer and her biggest supporter. She was born here in 1907 and lived here on and off throughout her life . . . as did her on-and-off husband, Mexican muralist Diego Rivera. The Blue House became a museum after Frida's death in 1954, but it still feels like she and Diego might walk in the door at any moment . . .

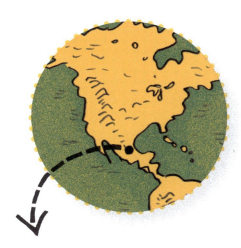

Bright blue walls intended to ward off evil spells, vibrant red floors, green windows . . . Frida wanted to create a house in her own image, radiating vitality and joy.

Who was Diego Rivera?
A famous Mexican painter (1886–1957) known for his large-scale murals and revolutionary politics. In 1929, he married Frida, a fellow artist and revolutionary. She was twenty-two; he was forty-two. They would both love and torment each other all their lives.

Who was Frida Kahlo?
A Mexican artist (1907-1954) and . . . a legend! Her strong personality and independence, and her short, passionate life—spent both in Mexico and in the US—are as fascinating as her often heart-wrenching paintings, known for their dreamlike magical realism.

★ Insider Tip
After his death, Diego Rivera left La Casa Azul to the Mexican people, and today it is financed solely through donations and ticket sales.

An Incredible Discovery
After Frida's death, Diego Rivera locked up thousands of her intimate belongings in a Blue House bathroom: traditional Mexican dresses, jewelry, letters, photos, books, her favorite red lipstick, hand-painted medical corsets . . . and instructions to leave it untouched until long after his death. Fifty years later, in 2004, her collection was unveiled. It took four years for the small museum team to organize it all, but now we have a deeper insight into Frida Kahlo, her tastes, her devotion to Mexico and to Communism, and her courage in the face of a lifetime of enormous physical challenges.

Face-to-Face

When Frida was only eighteen, she was in a terrible bus accident that broke her back, leaving her bedridden for months and in pain for life. To express herself — and to survive — she began to paint. Her mother mounted a mirror on the ceiling of her four-poster bed, allowing her to see her face and draw herself. About a third of Frida Kahlo's paintings are self-portraits..

▶ **Don't Miss . . .**
Stop into the kitchen with the lemon-yellow furniture and imagine the aromatic clay pots simmering on the wood-burning stove. Frida and Diego enjoyed spicy Mexican dishes like the mole negro of Oaxaca: chicken cooked in a sauce made of chocolate and chiles.

A Fashion Statement

Frida Kahlo was proud of her mixed heritage. Her father was German-born, and her mother — born in Oaxaca, Mexico — was of mixed Spanish and Indigenous descent. Frida's fierce pride in her Mexican identity was reflected in both her artwork and her flamboyant fashion choices, on display to admire at La Casa Azul.

- Crown of flowers
- Mayan jade necklace
- Traditional Mexican fringed shawl (rebozo)
- Shalimar perfume (Guerlain)
- Mexican earrings
- Flouncy long skirt

🔍 Working Behind the Scenes: Angel, Book Conservator

Frida and Diego were avid readers, and Angel's job is to preserve the books in their library. He stitches the loose pages, removes water stains, and reinforces tired bindings. His important work prolongs the life of these books, books that bear witness to the couple's many shared interests: poetry, history, science, and politics.

THE AMERICAN MUSEUM OF NATURAL HISTORY IN NEW YORK CITY
Earth's marvels on display

Exhibiting dinosaurs is no small feat, because it requires very tall ceilings! That's no problem for the American Museum of Natural History in New York City. Under the lofty vault of the Theodore Roosevelt Rotunda, a classic Jurassic battle plays out: a long-necked herbivore defends its young from an attacking allosaurus, a fearsome carnivorous reptile. Welcome to one of the finest dinosaur museums on Earth! This grand monument to the natural world is home to thousands of dinosaur fossils, including those from the stegosaurus, the triceratops, and even the famous T. rex.

These impressive collections continue to expand, thanks to numerous expeditions financed by the museum. Staff paleontologists gladly abandon their offices to survey deserts and mountains, relentlessly scouring the sand and rock in search of fossils. Who knows, maybe these field trips will push their research a big diplodocus's step further? Recently, an unknown species was unearthed in Argentina's Patagonia: the gigantic titanosaur. Its cast skeleton has been reconstructed in a room at the museum that barely contains it — the head sticks out into the corridor next door! At more than 122 feet (37 meters) long, it is one of the largest dinosaurs ever discovered. For now, anyway . . .

THE AMERICAN MUSEUM OF NATURAL HISTORY

faces Manhattan's beautiful Central Park, the giant green space of the city. It's one of the oldest museums in New York—opening in 1877—and one of the largest. The museum's neoclassical entrance welcomes you to its oldest gems and its newest wing: the Richard Gilder Center for Science, Education, and Innovation . . . with an insectarium, butterfly vivarium, and much more.

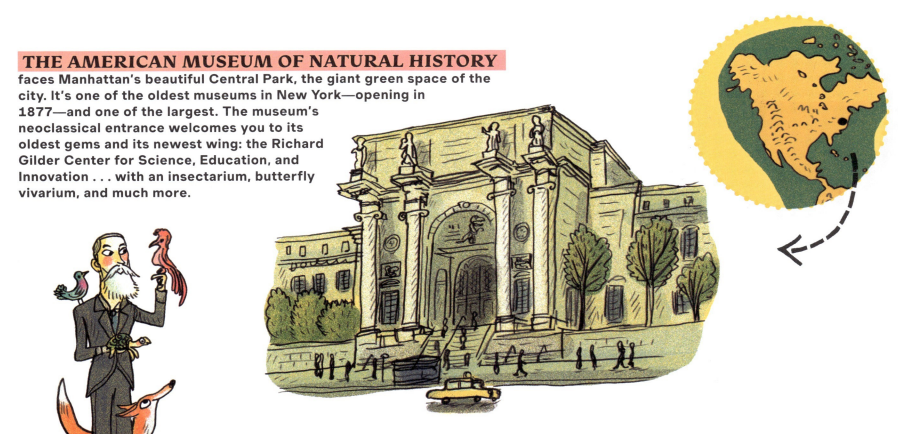

Who was Albert Bickmore?
He was the American man behind the museum. Born in 1839 in coastal Maine (in the United States), Albert was obsessed with science from early childhood when he studied marine life and collected shells. After his studies, he became a respected zoologist and fought to establish a major science museum in New York. His dream came true: The museum was built, and he became one of its first curators.

Real Life or . . . Diorama?

The museum houses many marvels beyond its world-famous mammoth skeleton and dinosaurs: minerals, meteorites, and, of course, the very special wildlife dioramas. You'll find these inviting landscapes behind glass, where the hidden worlds of wild animals in their natural habitats are revealed in lifelike, meticulously detailed artistic reconstructions. The dioramas are always a favorite, but they were particularly popular one hundred years ago when they gave New Yorkers the chance to travel to faraway lands without ever leaving home.

▶ **Don't Miss . . .**
The *Spectrum of Life* in the Hall of Biodiversity teems with fifteen-hundred specimens and models: insects, reptiles, mammals, birds, fish, and plants. This glass installation is 100 feet (30 meters) long, and showcases the astonishing diversity of life on Earth and the evolution of species spanning 3.5 billion years.

A Whale of an Honor

The museum also offers the Richard Gilder Graduate School, a PhD program in Comparative Biology. On graduation day, the students experience the perfect send-off: They receive their hard-won diplomas in the Hall of Ocean Life under the splendid blue whale, a life-sized reconstruction of the largest animal on Earth.

The Great Canoe

The Northwest Coast Hall, dedicated to Native Nations of the Pacific Northwest, has been renovated with the participation of tribal descendants in the US and Canada. A must-see: the large nineteenth-century Haida and Heiltsuk dugout canoe, sculpted from a single western red cedar tree, 63 feet (20 meters) long. What's happening here? Tribal members are honoring the Great Canoe with downy eagle feathers.

★ Insider Tip

American sculptor James Earle Fraser's Theodore Roosevelt statue that greeted visitors for eighty-plus years was removed in 2022 for its controversial "hierarchical composition." The bronze statue portrayed US President Theodore Roosevelt (1901–1909) on horseback, with African and Native figures walking alongside him.

Origami Tree

During the holidays, the museum displays an origami tree, decorated with hundreds of colorful creatures hand-folded by origami artists. In 2023, the tree's theme was "Proboscideans on Parade," inspired by the temporary exhibition *The Secret World of Elephants*.

Movie Magic

Even if you live thousands of miles from New York City, you can get a great look inside the museum by watching the 2006 film *Night at the Museum* — and its sequels. In the movie, a night security guard (played by Ben Stiller) thinks he's landed a nice, quiet job, but instead he finds himself embroiled in a wild adventure. Us, too!

🔎 Working Behind the Scenes: Nancy Simmons, Curator, Department of Mammalogy

Nancy is wild about the world's only flying mammals: bats. She studies chiropterans that lived millions of years ago to see how they evolved, and takes international field trips regularly. That's how she helped discover a new bat species with bright orange fur in the Nimba mountains of West Africa. Congratulations to this fearless scientist!

Monday isn't just another day at the Quai Branly . . . because it's closed on Mondays! There's not a single visitor in sight, but the museum is alive and humming anyway. The conservators take advantage of the peace and quiet to roam around inspecting their galleries' collections: statues, jewelry, clothing, and more, from four geographical areas: Africa, the Americas, Asia, and Oceania (which includes Australia plus the Central and South Pacific islands). One expert lovingly dusts off a Papuan mask with a brush. A North American specialist examines the headdress of a long-ago Sioux chief, to make sure no insects took up residence in its feathers.

A little farther away, in the conservation workshop, things are hopping, too. With her shiny gold boots and pink hair, Stéphanie is the resident fairy of this ultra-modern lab. Perched near the museum's halls, she's perfectly situated to find and repair any damaged treasures. Her team recently got their hands on nearly 150 musical instruments, many of them old and rare. Once the prized objects are back in tip-top shape, they'll be returned to the glass, six-floors-tall musical instrument tower where visitors can behold rows of timpani (kettledrums), tam-tams (gongs), balafons (gourd xylophones), bells, and harps. It's like a gigantic, soundless orchestra, keeper of all the songs of the world.

THE QUAI BRANLY MUSEUM opened its doors in Paris in 2006 when Jacques Chirac was president of France. He dreamed of a museum that would celebrate the art of non-European people. Construction began in 2001 along the Seine River, on "le quai Branly," the museum's location and namesake. French architect Jean Nouvel designed the long, bridge-like building with walls that hugged the curve of the river, just low enough to avoid casting a shadow on the Eiffel Tower.

The Quai Branly has a delightful vertical garden, or "living wall" of fifteen thousand plants, designed by French botanist Patrick Blanc.

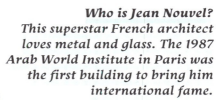

Who is Jean Nouvel? This superstar French architect loves metal and glass. The 1987 Arab World Institute in Paris was the first building to bring him international fame.

Aboriginal Paintings

The Quai Branly is not merely a building, it's a work of art. To further beautify it, Aboriginal painters created works for several walls and ceilings . . . even for the museum's roof. To see Western Australian (Gija) artist Lena Nyadbi's fishy *Barramundi Scales* from above, there is a trick: Climb the nearby Eiffel Tower and look down!

Spanning the Globe

A spiraling ramp leads up from the museum's entrance hall to a cavernous open space, the "Plateau des Collections," where thirty-five hundred objects are illuminated in the darkness. As visitors wander through Oceania and Asia, Africa and the Americas, cultures and civilizations are revealed through objects like clothing and photos but also through songs and films. Here are four not-to-be-missed masterpieces:

Ivory Coast chief's ornament (Africa)

Kanak mask, New Caledonia (Oceania)

Japanese samurai armor (Asia)

Bear totem pole, British Columbia (the Americas)

A Special Favorite
One prestigious collection inherited by the Quai Branly was gifted by the Musée de l'Homme (the Museum of Mankind), in Paris. The museum also buys works of art, like La Chupícuaro, this two-thousand-year-old terracotta Mexican statuette. (Its image is often used as a symbol of the museum.)

▶ Don't Miss . . .
Visit the gorgeous gardens—it's free! In this lush tangle, European ferns mingle with Japanese magnolias. The Quai Branly is built on stilts, so the gardens not only surround the museum, they also creep beneath it. Look out for scheduled storytelling, concerts, and workshops here, too.

A Most Unusual Library
Hidden away at the museum is a staff-only materials library that stockpiles bone fragments, skins, feathers, seeds, shells, and even porcupine quills. Here, conservation apprentices can check out these samples to learn more about the unique historical objects in the Quai Branly.

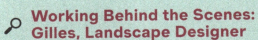

★ Insider Tip
A reading room surrounded by giant bamboo is open to visitors! Leaf through comics and manga—and the latest museum exhibition catalogs.

🔍 Working Behind the Scenes: Gilles, Landscape Designer
Ever since he was a child, Gilles has enjoyed getting his hands dirty. He's fascinated by nature and has made it his job: He creates ecological gardens like the Quai Branly's, which he designed from A to Z, choosing plants from the four corners of the world that could easily adapt to the Parisian climate. He believes in letting plants grow at their own pace; the gardener is only there to watch over them like a caring, unintrusive parent. One day, you might spot him at the Quai Branly, checking to see how his gardens are evolving through the years and seasons.

Acknowledgments:
Thanks to all the museum professionals who helped or inspired the writing of this book, and, in particular: Gianni Crea, Lucia Agirre, Maria Fernandez Sabau, Idoia Arrate, Aitor, Philippe Fouchard, Charlotte Lescale, Marianne Kuhn, Cécile Dumoulin, Angeliki Galanaki, Muriel Filleul, Barbara Lepêcheux, Marie-Charlotte Calafat, Hélène Taam, Dorine and Tianshu, Isabelle de Vielleville, Marion Benaiteau, Olivier Brunel, Eric Lefebvre, Stéphanie Elarbi, Alexandre Holin, Christel Moretto, Gaëlle de Bernède, Federica Facchetti. And let's not forget a few caresses for Louchka, Mavrik, and Charlotka, the Hermitage cats.

–Éva Bensard

Thanks to my godmother, Ariane Adriani, who opened the doors of museums for me.

–Benjamin Chaud

Thank you to the staff at the Smithsonian Institution and the American Museum of Natural History for contributions to their respective sections of this publication.

–Red Comet Press

CREDITS
The illustrations in this book were based on the works of ancient and modern artists.
The following works are protected by copyright:

At the Guggenheim Museum Bilbao
For the museum building, designed by Frank Gehry (1997): © Architectural Works by Gehry Partners, LLP.
For the work *Maman* by Louise Bourgeois (1999): © The Easton Foundation / Adagp, Paris 2023.
For the work *Puppy* by Jeff Koons (1992): © Jeff Koons.
For the work *The Matter of Time* by Richard Serra (1994–2005): © Adagp, Paris, 2023.

At the Mucem in Marseille
For the museum building, designed by Rudy Ricciotti and Roland Carta (2013): © Architects Rudy Ricciotti and Roland Carta / Mucem.
For the garden: © Agence APS - Jardin des Migrations / Mucem.

At the Quai Branly museum in Paris
For the museum building, designed by Jean Nouvel (2006): © Jean Nouvel / Musée du Quai Branly / Adagp, Paris, 2023.

The Great Big Book of Museums
First English language edition published in 2025 by Red Comet Press, LLC, Brooklyn, NY
Translation by Karin Snelson
English text © 2025 Red Comet Press

Originally published as *Le grand livre des musées*
French text © 2023 Éditions Arola / Éva Bensard
Illustrations © 2023 Éditions Arola / Benjamin Chaud
Copyright © 2023 Éditions Arola

The edition was published by arrangement with The Picture Book Agency, France

All rights reserved. No part of this book may be used or reproduced in any manner whatsoever without written permission except in the case of brief quotations embodied in critical articles and reviews.

Library of Congress Control Number: 2024951279
ISBN (HB): 978-1-63655-152-4
ISBN (Ebook): 978-1-63655-153-1

25 26 27 28 29 30 TLF 10 9 8 7 6 5 4 3 2 1

Red Comet Press is distributed by ABRAMS, New York
Manufactured in China

RedCometPress.com

Find links and more information about each of the museums at the QR code or at
redcometpress.com/nonfiction/museums

ÉVA BENSARD is a graduate of the Louvre School. She is a freelance journalist for art magazines, and also writes nonfiction books for young readers specializing in art and architecture. She is the author of *Amazing Artworks: The World's Biggest, Oldest, Most Jaw-Dropping Creations*. Her mission is to make art accessible to everyone — in her books, poetry, and travels, art and history happily coexist. Éva Bensard lives and works in Paris, France.

BENJAMIN CHAUD is one of the most renowned French illustrators. He has illustrated more than seventy picture books, including *101 Ways to Read a Book* written by Timothée de Fombelle and published by Red Comet Press. He is the author and illustrator of *New York Times* Notable Book *The Bear's Song* and three sequels. He is also the illustrator of *A Funny Thing Happened at the Museum* written by his frequent collaborator Davide Calì. Benjamin Chaud lives in the south of France.